A S

C000314755

Sentence

Karl Loxton

Table Of Contents

Acknowledgments

This book is dedicated to...

My mum and dad. I would not be alive today without your love, guidance and support, which I treasure and value each and every day.

My children, Iwan and Leona. You and your journeys inspire me daily and are my motivation to always keep going. I love you both with all I have.

My bro, Huw. I love you more than words can say each and every day.

My extended family, whose faith and hope in me never wavered. I love you all.

My friend Clive - you are a rock, a football friend and an all-round great guy.

To all those who have helped me through this journey - too many to mention individually but each valued equally, from medical staff, to prison officers, friends close by to friends afar, I will always remember the part you played on my journey.

To Helen for believing in, reading and typing up my work - what a journey it has been! Thank you for your guidance, support and the time you gave willingly and freely to turn my little book into print.

Michelle, a special thank you to you my friend. For always believing in my writing, encouraging me to share and above all, whether nearby or far away, being a most amazing friend, and for showing the power of friendship every single day over many years.

Your friendship made this book possible and I thank you from the heart for that.

And lastly to Peggy, an incredible lady, who has taught me so much. You inspire me, with your wit, enthusiasm and outlook on life. I hope I still have the approach to life you have, if I'm lucky enough to live in years, the years you have lived. Thank you Peggy, for being you.

About The Author

Hi, I'd like to start by thanking you for taking the time to delve into my book.

So I'll be honest, this has been the hardest page to write!!! But here's a little bit about me. I was a teacher in a primary and then a special educational needs setting until

2016 when I retired due to ill health. After retiring I struggled to come to terms with aspects of my life and in 2021 I was sent to prison. Whilst in prison I had the chance to process my life, seek forgiveness and find ways to help myself. One of those ways was writing, and A Short Sentence is the self help writing journey I went on in prison. I was released from prison in April 2022 and am slowly rebuilding my life. Today, I have so much to be grateful for including my children, family and friends. I continue to write, to help manage the challenges of daily life. Aside from writing I enjoy taking photos, walking, escaping with my music, and the time I get with, and the love of my family and friends.

Reviews of A Short Sentence

"I told you its amazing!!! I know it will be a best seller, once you start reading you can't put it down" xx

Black, M.

"I'm really enjoying reading your book. It's very stirring, awe inspiring, emotional,

impressive, heart warming and evokes such empathy, compassion and strength. It shows your

strength through so much adversity and your determination through hard times that helped pull you through.

Your love of your family and friends and the enjoyment you get from writing has certainly helped massively.

I'm in awe and totally respect you Karl. Thank you for being so honest throughout, and for

sharing not just your words but your poems. They will certainly help others, of that I'm sure.

It must have been very cathartic writing all of this. Bravo!"

Parry, A

"It's certainly a thought provoking, insightful and emotional read. I felt like I had been on the journey with you, just by typing it out!!!

Lawton, H.

My Mum

We all have a mum,

Mine is truly number one!

Whenever I need someone to care,

For over 48 years, mum's been right there.

If I've done something to make her frown, instead she hugs me to calm me down.

She has dealt with many challenges in her life, but has always been an amazing mum and wife.

So, on your special "Mother's Day"

I just want the chance to say...

Thank you for all you do, guiding me along life's way.

Mothering Sunday 2022

"The greatest wealth you can ever have is
to find peace with your own mental
health"

13/3/22

Preface

I arrived at HMP Oakwood on 9th June 2021. This was to be my first and (fingers crossed!) last sentence.

I was sent down on Friday 23rd April 2021 and by the time I arrived at Oakwood I was at the third prison in just over 6 and a half weeks.

It was here that I truly broke. I battled depression, bouts of self – harm and very serious thoughts of another suicide attempt. But this is not a journey of fear and sadness, it's about the journey I went on and the short sentence that changed my life forever. It's about how I found a way to express myself and use that expression to set myself free.

I first received counselling in 2014. After two sessions, my father- in- law's cancer returned and three weeks later I lost an incredibly important man from my life. I tried to be strong for others by returning to work and supporting my family, but a series of unfortunate events then took place.

A car crashed in front of me on the way home from work one evening. I stopped to help and to my horror, it was a young man I knew! Sadly, he died, leaving a fiancée and unborn child. I knew her well, as her mum lived opposite me. Speaking at the inquiry was so very hard, but I said I was ok and didn't want to talk with anyone about what I had seen, as I felt such guilt that I could not save him, even though I knew there was nothing more I could do.

Next, I was rushed into hospital to have my appendix removed.

In September 2015, I walked out of the school I was working at on a Friday afternoon, dragged myself to the doctor's the following Monday and never set foot in a classroom again. Two weeks later I started on antidepressants and one year later I was retired from teaching on the grounds of mental ill health. I was forty-three.

In conversations I was told how lucky I was. I took it all without ever saying anything. Deep down, I was broken. I felt like I was a burden, definitely nothing about my life seemed lucky.

Life became more challenging at home as I took on the role of stay at home dad. Things were not easy, I became closed off and felt that there was an expectation for me to be ok, even though deep down I felt a failure and completely dead inside.

Fast forward to April 2019, when I made the decision to take my own life. It was the worst five months of my life. I started to gamble with money which was not mine. I hoped to win enough so that my family would be ok and in a better position financially when I was dead. As you can imagine, this did not end well, but still I felt that I couldn't share with anyone how I was feeling.

On 31st August 2019 I drove to a wood and tried to overdose. A little light stopped me, it kept reflecting in my wing mirror and would not let me go. I drove home, knowing I was going to have to face the consequences of my actions. But, I believed so strongly in the light that I saw because it seemed to want me to be alive.

That same day, I was asked to leave the family home. I never went back. My parents collected me and were totally shocked at my appearance and demeanour. I broke that night as I told them and my brother all that had happened in the previous five months. I felt shame, fear, failure and more. They didn't judge me, they called hospitals and GPs and, on the Monday, I started to get the help I needed.

I was arrested and later given a custodial sentence. I was divorced and I had lost contact with my children.

I accept all those things. Whilst in prison, I finally disclosed the sexual abuse I had suffered when I was fourteen years old.

This was not for any other reason but to forgive the younger version of myself. I was humbled by how the police treated me through this and when I was able to identify my abuser, now deceased, the young Karl shed a tear for me, as I shed tears for him.

This little book has been formed out of my musings in a journal I won in a poetry competition and kept with me to record my journey in prison. I always wondered if one day I would share my journey. That day has arrived. I know it's right because in sharing my journey it has helped me to heal, find peace and just be me.

PART ONE

Karl's Quotes

"Whilst you have air in your lungs and hope in your heart, it is never too late to ask for help"

13/10/21

"To live is to be alive, which is far more important than to understand all that happens in life"   14/10/21

"Some people say that crying is a weakness. If that's true then I embrace my weakness as I would rather cry and survive, than be silent and die"

15/10/21

"Never underestimate the power of meeting the most amazing, caring and empathetic people, in the most unlikely circumstances you would ever expect to find yourself in!"   22/10/21

"LIFE- Love In Friend's Empathy. Something that is always worth living for, as amazing friends change lives forever"

4/11/21

"If mental illness turned my skin green, would you react differently because you could see something was wrong with me?!!"

5/11/21

"Difficult days make amazing days possible!"

8/11/21

"The most exciting part of closing a difficult chapter in your life, is the opening of a fresh, blank page, waiting- clean, new and ready just for you"

9/11/21

"Recovery is not about returning to you; it's about finding what you need to recover your soul"

11/11/21

"Anxiety is over – rated. Hope most definitely is NOT"

17/11/21

"Some days you just have to lock yourself away and say "Not today, world"- and believe me, that's ok"

18/11/21

"Kindness is doing something that you want to, no praise needed. The reward is the glow that comes from the act of kindness"

30/11/21

"You have the power within you to change minds and lives: But first make sure you use that power to make your own mind and life as kind as it can be!"

19/12/21

"Magical moments can only be found by surviving and staying alive"

5/1/22

"The greatest gift you can offer another human is to listen, really listen and freely give them your time"

18/1/22

PART TWO

A Few Short Poems

The Mirror

Look in the mirror and what do you see?

I see the person that will allow me to live and be free.

And the person I see?

That person is ME!

13/10/21

Depression

Depression for me is like being a ship,

Unable to dock, as waves crash all around, crushing me in the teeth of the storm.

I know what I need to do, but it's oh so hard!

I must do it, fight the storm of my mind
and find a place to dock.

Find a safe port of call where I can set
down my anchor, rest and ride out the

storm.

With people I know who really care.

26/10/21

Keys

Clunk, clink, prison keys.

Fear spreads as they jangle past.

Don't click in my door!

28/10/21

Who Are You?

Who are you to judge me?

What do you think you see?

Do you think you know about me?

I will tell you what you see?

You see what I allow you to see.

You see my outer, protective shell.

You see the smile that easily hides pain.

But you don't see my internal scars.

Until you really take time to know me

walk on by, and don't comment on what you think you see.

Save your judgement for someone other than me.

What you have judged me on is what you can see, or think you see.

That is such a small percentage of me.

So, I finish as I started by asking...

Who are you to really judge me?

You are no-one until you really know me!

4/11/21

The Room

I walk into a crowded room with a broken leg.

At once, people flock around me to ask, "What happened?"

They offer kind words, help and well wishes.

I walk into the same crowded room,

riddled with nerves, anxiety and a little panic.

At once, no-one flocks to me, those same people don't even notice me.

That's hidden illness, whatever it be, it can't be helped. I can't help that you can't see it, can't help the fact my illness is unseen.

But…. Am I not still that same, one person each time I walk into that room?

5/11/21

Living

As I look outside,

My eyes open and smile inside,

Grateful I'm alive.

18/11/21

The Library

I was lost before.

I'm now free, thanks to the Library,

Colleagues, books and more.

25/11/21

White Out

Wow, snow everywhere!

I hope my pylon is ok!

For he, I don't see.

27/11/21

Not Again!

It's more Covid woe!

Behind doors for hours once more.

Let's hope it's sorted soon!

27/12/21

I'm Oh So Scared!

I'm oh, so scared of what's to come!

My emotions and mood swings often leaving me feeling numb.

One minute I feel absolutely fine.

The next I am plunged into the depths of despair, fearful of the passage of time.

I try to stay positive for all to see;

But once the cell door closes, it's just the darkness and me.

Emotionally exhausted all of the time,

I stay in my cell and hide away. I'm oh, so scared of what's to come!

28/12/21

PART THREE
Personal Thoughts Blog

Numb, Sweaty and Finally Free

I woke this morning, drenched in sweat, feeling numb and hot to my inner core. But, alongside these physical symptoms, I also had symptoms of joy, relief and feelings of a final freedom.

Yesterday afternoon, after thirty-four years, I was shown a series of photographs. Instantly, I recognised the man. Looking at me from these photos was the man who had sexually assaulted me.

They say no one forgets a face; I certainly hadn't forgotten his! Seeing it, after all those years evoked many feelings and emotions. However, more than anything, was an over riding feeling that a door was finally closing on that chapter of my life.

I had done exactly what I had set out to do, I had found and made peace with my younger self. By finally reporting my abuse, I had found a way to forgive myself, so that I could face my life without constantly looking back over my shoulder.

I have made my peace, set my emotions free from their captor and as a result no longer does he roam the thoughts in my mind. It really is never too late to "own your own shit"- In finding the strength to talk- it really is never too late to find your voice.

19/10/21

Like The Daily Sun Rise

The sun always rises, just as it sets at the end of each day. We don't always see this, but we know it does. As this happens daily, so we are given the chance to be alive, as daily the sun sustains life on Earth, the place we call home.

I have learnt from the sun, that however challenging each day is, we still have the chance to rise and manage that day. If you do this, then when you rise on your positive, sunny days, you will feel the warmth on your back and your smile will shine as brightly as the sun itself! On your less positive, dark, damp, dreary days, you will still rise and you will travel through this difficult day, just like the sun.

So, take hope and heart from our sun and you will find a way to get through. Rise, be as one with our sun on all your days, be it dark and damp or bright and beautiful.

4/11/21

Support

Support is given and promised in many ways, but for me, the key to support is that the person that offers it remembers to give it. Today a line manager remembered their commitment to offer support by checking in with me. She said it would be about 2 weeks until that check- in and it was. The worth of that support, both offered and given is a priceless commodity.

Actions are such powerful things and although on the face of it, todays check- in was a small gesture, it was so much more than that to me. I was given time, a chance to be listened to and as importantly heard. That, to me, is the true value of support. I am thankful that she took time out of her day to offer support to me.

I hope, one day, that I can do the same for someone who needs to be seen, heard and listened to.

14/11/21

The Sea, My Mum, Depression And Me

Butterflies in my stomach, sweat pouring
from my brow, the rushing tide stalks
dark thoughts locked within my mind.
Panting, breathless, nowhere to run, I'm
dragged under as anxiety drives my mind
numb. Swept by currents from within my
mind, I gasp for breath. My lungs fill with
water, right now it's hope I must find.

Has my depression won?

Is my race run?

Suddenly sea waves sweep me up. It's
empowering, wrapped in relief, like
Mum's arms filled with love, cradling me
reassuringly. Carefully, gently, I'm placed

upon the sand. My Mum's sea waves guiding me lovingly, to safety.

Challenges

We are often met with challenges that we don't see coming. They can play on both our mind and nerves. Allow them to play on your mind, but make sure that you are in charge of the tune that each challenge plays. By doing this, you can and will overcome the challenge you have been set, as you make the challenge play to the beat of your tune. The beat that says, "Challenge accepted, challenge tackled, challenge met, now a challenge no more!" The challenge is met because only you can play and overcome the playlist of your mind. So, make sure your playlist allows

your mind to tackle each challenge to the
tune and beat you set!!

13/12/21

Acceptance

You can and will cope with all life has to
throw at you, especially when you allow
acceptance to enter your heart, mind and
thoughts. I know, that in accepting me for
who I am, inside and out, means that I am
a kinder, happier person.

Today, instead of fearing life, I know I
want to live it and accept all it has to
offer.

19/12/21

A Child's Love

Yesterday evening I spoke with my daughter. It was a lovely way to end my Christmas day. We laughed and talked about being able to FaceTime each other in 2022 once I'm released from prison.

She then said to me, "Dad, promise me one thing."

Followed by, "I know you struggle with your mental health and in the past you have tried to kill yourself, but promise me you won't again, my life would be so hard to live if my dad wasn't in it!"

Wow! I was blown away by the understanding, openness and honesty she showed. I don't exactly know what kept me alive on that fateful day in August 2019. I just knew that whatever hardship was to come, I just had to face it and keep on going.

I now know why, it was to follow the light I saw on that day and to keep going for future brightness, hope and love. What could be brighter than the love and faith my daughter has shown in me?

25/12/21

Closing '21

Well, what a year it has been! It is said that what doesn't break you makes you stronger and this last year has certainly tested that theory for me!

I could go on and list all the events of 2021, but they have been and gone. However, one thing I have learnt more than anything else is not to look backwards at your past with loathing, fear and failure. Instead, I have learnt to turn around, face the road ahead and be proud. Be proud of who you are, after all, without your past you can't be your present you. If you are present, then anything is possible! Why? Because you believed in yourself enough to keep going, despite those challenges of your past.

For this lesson I am grateful. Here's to each new day! Own your past! Live for the now! Believe in yourself and you will see that all your hopes and dreams really can come true!

31/12/21

Keep Going- You Will be Heard

Some days you may feel unheard, neglected even, as if no-one can see that you are mentally suffering despite your pleas for help. It can be the most awful feeling and the world can close in very rapidly.

At that point, my advice is, keep asking and talking. Remember, you have come this far, you deserve to be heard. Trust in the fact that eventually someone will hear your cries and act on what you are saying.

I know this, as it happened to me. I managed to keep on asking today and eventually a Wing Officer heard my request. At first, it was declined.

A short while later, the Officer came back and granted me the five minutes I had asked for to leave my cell, just to help me manage my mental state at that point in time.

It was empowering for me. I was heard and as a result I was able to move on with my day, proud of the fact that I hadn't given up, I had kept on asking until I was heard.

12/1/22

Patience

I made my regular, weekly call to my daughter on Tuesday 4th January 2022.

I was happily chatting away with her, when I heard a voice say, "Hello, dad!"

I could hardly believe it, this was the first time I had heard my son's voice for nine months!

My daughter stayed on the phone, put it on speakerphone for us and we had a three-way chat for about forty minutes! On saying goodbye, I was ecstatic!

I shed tears of joy. I had exercised patience and when my son felt ready he had reached out to me.

Since that call, my son has messaged my mum, so that she could pass on his mobile number to the prison to allow it to be added to my approved prison numbers.

I had to wait a week for the approval, but now I have it! Yesterday evening we chatted for over an hour. Moving forward, it has been arranged that I will ring him weekly.

What a wonderful position I now find myself in because I found a way to stay patient!

18/1/22

The Healing Library

Today I am back in the prison library and I feel such joy. It is the place where I am at my best, a place I am able to be myself, as I work my way through daily tasks.

Certain events, times and places shape your life's journey. For me, during my time in HMP Oakwood, the library has been that place. It has offered me the things I need on that journey and much more. Most of all, it has given me the time and sent me the people I needed to allow myself to heal.

It's where I feel at home. I work with amazing people that genuinely care and as a result, my mental health has improved beyond anything I ever thought possible.

As I get ready to return there, following a month's absence due to a nasty bout of Covid 19, I have had time to think about what I want to say.

It's an easy task for me! It's a massive thank you to Meg, Claire, Julie and Sue, for helping me find ME again! I will never forget the time spent in the Healing Library.

19/1/22

PART FOUR
Longer Poems

The Library

I work as an orderly,

In the prison library.

I am at my happiest there,

Because I'm surrounded by people who

care.

The staff just welcomed me as ME!

And this has become the magical key.

I've been allowed to find myself,

Surrounded by books improved my
mental health.

Meg, Julie, Sue and Claire

Have opened my eyes to a place where...

Hopes, dreams, fears and more

Are looked after by stepping through the door.

I will be sad when it's my time to go,

But the library will be remembered always with a warm glow.

2/2/22

Broken, Shattered Thoughts

Right now, I feel completely broken,

I hope tomorrow I can't be woken!

I sit down here, alone in my cell,

Knowing that life's just not going well.

My brain is full of despair and dread,
voices chastise me within my head.

I look for a way to distract my mind, from
the thoughts saying, "Karl, leave this life
behind!"

The distraction I find is self-harm,

Cuts I make to each arm,

It hurts, it throbs, it draws a tear;

But momentarily the pain distracts my
hidden fear.

Every bone weighted, as if filled with lead,
I finally find a way to crawl into bed.

Duvet pulled tightly up to hide away,

My world is dark both night and day.

Silently, I start to weep,

AS desperately I wish for sleep.

I pray to find one sleep token,

No need for any words to be spoken.

Closing my eyes, still and battered,

Life in pieces, completely shattered.

7/7/21

Pressing the Cell Bell

Pressing the cell bell, almost impossible
to do.

Thoughts rush through my mind, "How
will it reflect on me?"

I press it, the battle rages in my mind,

"What will happen as the door opens and
the officer sees me behind?"

Will I be judged for the war in my head?

Right now, not caring,

Better than thoughts of dread!

An officer came, the door unlocked,

"You ok?"

"No" I replied, as I went off half- cocked.

My emotions poured out, like a tap
running fast,

The officer listened patiently, until I finished ranting at last.

Then she spoke and I just knew at once she had heard,

The relief was like flying, free as a bird!

I found myself living my own mental hell, until I decided to press that cell bell.

I'm now so grateful that I did,

No more thoughts suppressed and hid.

I'll continue this battle to stay alive and well,

Forever grateful I pressed the cell bell.

23/8/21

The Pylon

I live on the 4's at HMP Oakwood, a room with a view between the bars.

I'm grateful that there are things to see, challenging my mind, to keep isolation at bay.

From the window I notice many things, including trains that race on by.

I've loved trains for many a year.   As they fly by, I think of dad, and the times spent watching them when I was a young lad.

I've developed a fascination, driven by imagination, As I view a structure I call Pylon.

Pylon is so strong and tall, with four metal legs rooted to the floor.

So much my pylon would share if he could, move from that place, that is his permanent resting base.

Pylon and I often chat,

(well, it's more he listens as I rattle on!)

I often wonder what pylon would say?

If only he could find a way.

I look into his eyes and a sadness I do see,
it feels so raw, it truly touches me.

I wonder how many people have seen my
pylon? From trains? From cars? From the
view I have?

Many, I'm sure, have glanced across.

Do they give him a thought?

I doubt it, as life is one big rush!

To them I'm sure he is just a piece of
metal, to me, he's a giant trapped by legs
of steel.

Pylon is outside, I am in, our shared bond
is that neither of us can roam free!

I look across and wonder, "Can he hear me?"

I hope he can as he's become my friend.

The strength it takes to stand so tall,

Carrying power, for all.

I shed a tear, I want my pylon to know,

I see his strength, draw on his power,

And use it to grow.

As the day starts, I look, I smile,

I take a moment to thank pylon for the power he has shown to me.

He carries an amazing gift, the current allowing me to read and write, helping my life find a flow.

I'm not sure my pylon can hear me, but I thank him and raise my cup of morning coffee.

Pylon gives comfort in so many ways,

I'm grateful for his power,

Hour after hour!

He can see what I see, for mile after mile,
in the moment.

What do our journeys hold?

Neither of us can know.

But with the strength I take from pylon, I
will walk my journey's path, And give it a
damn good go!

26/8/21

Pad Tossing

In they come,

Two of them.

No time to explain.

"We heard you might be hiding Hooch,

So, we are here to have a mooch!"

A couple of questions I was asked, my answers shaky, I hoped my fear was masked.

I knew I had nothing, I don't even drink!

But my head raced as I tried to think.

A minute or so later, cell tossing complete,

They closed the door and made their retreat.

I sit here now, wondering why? Not a thanks or a sorry, not even goodbye!

It's left me feeling stressed and sad,

And thinking, why would it be Hooch I had?

I guess that I will never know,

But the anxiety landed a heavy blow. The cell tossing was just a horrid session, which rapidly triggered a deep depression.

8/9/21

Feelings In My Cell

Helpless, hopeless, out of control,

Life in a cell has taken its toll.

Emotions wash over me every day,

I struggle to keep my fears at bay.

Family, friends, it's all on pause,

Worst of all my head's saying that I'm the
cause.

I just hope when I'm finally home,

I will just feel much less alone!

I've felt that it's been all my fault,

So I crack and life crashes to a halt.

Not because I want to wave goodbye,

I'm scared that my friends won't want to
say Hi!

All's not lost, I'm finally realising I'm me,

I'm allowed to laugh, smile, cry, be okay

and feel free.

So, when I walk through those prison

gates, I hope those who really know me

will still be my mates.

6/10/21

Moving On

When all is said and done,

And you feel like your life is run,

Remember there is more to come,

And everyone deserves some fun!

You are not being asked to forget your

past, but no longer should you feel you

have to hide behind a mask.

What's done is done and already gone,

So, take a deep breath and remember,

You deserve to move on.

29/10/21

An Ode to Covid in Prison

I was dealt a bitter blow,

That test left me feeling incredibly low!

Positive was my Covid test,

So, my cell became my full-time nest.

Locked up 24/7 is extremely tough,

Especially when you feel so rough.

I've coughed, I've spluttered and so much more,

And at times felt ill to my very core.

But as 2022 is welcomed in,

Covid won't take me to the rubbish
bin!

So, let's raise a glass to the year ahead,

It's always better to be living than dead!

1/1/22

Today I Miss...

Walking with the freedom to explore.

My safe place at Borrowpit Lake and the
beauty it brings.

My phone to take photos and the joy that
I feel from it.

My flat, my sanctuary, my little place that
holds all I have.

Texts- I can't text Hi to my friends, nor
can they back to me.

The rushing water of the local river.

Meeting my parents for Sunday dinner and a chat.

Today, I miss these things and so much more,

As I sit on my own behind my prison cell door.

The sun shines radiantly in the blue winter sky,

But today I feel alone, a lonely middle aged guy.

I try to stay positive as I serve my time,

And I will always regret committing the crime.

But the biggest battle that I have to face,

Is 24-hour isolation in this place.

It enhances all I cherish and all that I miss,

But I picture the day I leave as my future bliss.

Till then I will keep going, each and every day,

No longer hiding my feelings or my illness away.

2/1/22

The Sparrow

"Chirp, chirp," I hear daily from my cell, the sound of nature, a sign that all is well.

The little sparrow lightens the mood, He sings and searches on the wing for food.

One moment he's resting safely on the bars up high, the next he's swooping swiftly on by.

The fellow seems to love our wing, And his daily visits, much joy they bring.

The window is open and in he flies! Putting on a show, as if to cheer up all the guys!

Sparrow has visited now for quite a while, showing us how nature will go the extra mile.

He's introduced us to robin, pigeon and more, thanks to him I smile when officers open up my door.

Wildlife just has that uplifting power, We roared when sparrow chased a con out of the shower!

So, never forget to look all around, because there's always nature's beauty to be found.

19/1/22

Forgiving To Embrace Living

I now look forward to life, with a smile.

Personal thoughts no longer put myself
on trial.

No more do I live in fear;

Anxious, frightened that suicide's near!

The present is just where I want to be,

As in each moment I'm proud to be me.

In seven months, my life has changed, No
longer do I feel ashamed.

I own my sadness and regrets, I've served
my time and paid my debts,

Thoughts and feelings, no longer I hide,
no more do mental battles destroy my
pride.

When at my worst I was stressed, anxious
and depressed, but kindness was found,
and I felt blessed.

No more is my life devoid and blank, For
that, there are many I wish to

thank.

They encouraged, heard and listened

at length, by showing patience and
kindness, I found my inner strength.

Which means that I can honestly say,
That every single air- filled day,

Is a chance to live, enjoy each breath, No
longer hoping for my own death.

By finally finding and allowing personal
forgiving,

I embrace my life,

So grateful I got the chance to go on living.

11/2/22

PART FIVE

February 2022 And Beyond!

This part starts with a poem I wrote as a way of thanking the Wing staff for all their support over the last eight months.

An Ode To CD Uppers Staff

For eight months my home has been CD
Uppers,

Where the staff work hard, no time for
cuppas!

Charlotte, Tonya, Mia, Gary, Brad the
usual staff.

Treat them with respect, you'll see they're
fair and enjoy a laugh!

But, it's very wise not to disagree, If you
do, don't moan about a negative IEP.

They try to help and solve all our probs,

Even finding toilet roll for use on the
bogs!

Don't take the piss with cell bell pressing,
After all, it's for emergencies, Not the
washing you need for dressing!

So, be wise and remember, they're on our
team,

And please be nice on Friday,

So we get our Canteen!

They know who's trying to sneak off on a
quick detour,

You know because they'll shout, "Behind
your door!"

Certain shouts you quickly learn to
recognise, like "servery", "five minutes!"
and "last chance for exercise!"

But always remember, they do their best,

Even when we challenge them and put them to the test!

So, as this Ode ends, I just want to say, Thank you so much for helping me find a way, to manage each and every Oakwood day!

22/2/22

Today, I had a letter from a friend - a friend who had been through their own challenges, but was now in a position to write and see how I was feeling. As a result of an exchange of letters I have now been able to phone them and came up with this quote abut listening.

"Finding someone who really listens is a powerful gift. Not because they have solutions to all of your problems, but by them actively listening, you feel heard. When life is closing in, being heard can make a difference that's impossible to put into words. "

22/3/22

"Just because you look ok, doesn't mean that you are! Just because you appeared to cope for weeks, doesn't mean that you are! So, instead of judging me on how I appear, actually ask me how I'm feeling - otherwise, how can you ever be sure I really am ok?"

24/3/22

"Never be afraid to offer help and support to others, but never offer if the price you pay is failing to help yourself"

30/3/22

The following blog is inspired by the book The Midnight Library by Matt Haig.

An absolutely brilliant, thought provoking book that has allowed me to find my inner Nora Seed, ultimately be me and enjoy my own midnight library on a daily basis.

Infinity, Me And The Midnight Library

Sometimes you have a moment, a moment where you see things with incredible clarity. This recently happened to me in a meeting, when I realised that I knew exactly why at this time I was reading The Midnight Library.

I could see exactly why I resonated with Nora Seed so very much. That moment of clarity will stay with me always.

Luckily, I didn't have to wait to get to my Midnight Library (the place between suicide and life or death), the place where you can try out your infinite, alternate lives before you live or die.

I don't have to wait, as it is right here, right now, each and every day, the choices I make, the routes I follow and the emotions that come with each individual choice. As I realised this, I physically felt a weight lift from me, I felt lighter, free and proud!

But why?

Because, within this lifetime I have already lived many lives. I've been married, divorced, a teacher, a parent and a prisoner. I've lived through pain, pain I will never, truly be able to explain. However, I've also lived through moments of incredible ecstasy, such as the birth of my son, the adoption of my daughter and the hug from a friend that says "I get you!"

So, to me, life is a type of infinity- it can be kind, it can be cruel, but it never stands still. Indeed, I must own previous choices made and those yet to be made because that is life. It is the chance to make and live infinite choices as I travel through this wonderful life journey.

31/3/22

HDC/ TAG Thoughts

Today, I found out that I've been provisionally granted HDC (Home Detention Curfew) This means I could be leaving prison in as little as 10 days' time!

It is hard to put into words all the feelings I have been experiencing since hearing the news. They include, excitement to get home, see my flat and video-call my kids! Also, the relief that potentially, my sentence could be coming to an end. I also have fear of stepping back into a world which I'm sure will have changed so much in the last twelve months and I worry that, for whatever reason, whilst out on TAG and then completing my sentence on License, I may fall foul of a recall to prison!

Having said that, all the potential feelings and emotions can only be experienced by grasping the opportunity to live daily because only in living can I see what happens next.

I want to finish this particular thoughts blog with a quote from The Midnight Library...

"Yesterday, I knew I had no future, and it was impossible for me to accept my life as it is now. And yet today that same messy life seems full of hope. Potential. The impossible, I suppose, happens via living" (The Midnight Library, Haig, Matt. 2020)

In essence, for me, whatever happens in life I can only see by living, experiencing and being accepting of myself which means that today and everyday, however hard it is, I will always choose life. Only by living can I experience what happens to me, and all of us are always worth living for as if we don't how will we ever know the experiences we could have had?

After all, if we don't, we will never find out what happens next in the Book of Life, the Book that you can only add chapters to, by living.

The previous blog was written a couple of days ago when I found out I'd been provisionally granted HDC.

It is now Sunday 3rd April and I have had forty-eight hours to digest the news. I have also re read the previous Blog entry and I am rather proud of it! Yes, I am anxious about leaving prison, but I also can't wait to see what the next chapter in my life brings. Because, whatever a chapter throws at you, if you have found acceptance in your own body and soul then you will find a way through, I did, and I truly believe that if I can, you can too!

3/4/22

So, assuming all goes to plan, I will be granted my HDC release on Monday 11th

April. In reality, that means I am entering my final week in HMP Oakwood. That thought has given me an idea. I am going to add a Final Chapter of emotions, thoughts and feelings as I progress through the week and my release gets closer. So, here it goes, with a very original title! The Final Chapter!

4/4/22

PART SIX

The Final Chapter

The Visit

A poem I wrote to reflect on my parents
final visit to see me.

Yesterday, I saw my parents, face to face!

It was lovely, but I hope it was their last
visit to my prison place.

Every month they came to see me
(Oakwood's not that near)

And each time I've been pleased, when
the LFD test's clear.

At first, visits made me feel guilty.
Visiting a prison to see me!

But, I've accepted over time, this was the
way, they wanted it to be.

A chance to catch up monthly,

To hug, smile and chat.

Hugs that carried an emotional, loving tight arm- wrap!

As restrictions eased, they were able to bring me some money.

This was cherished as I sipped and savoured, the latte warming my tummy!

But, most of all each visit allowed me to see, how much love, faith and belief they both still had in me.

So, what more can I say?

Thank you, mum and dad, for each visit, every catch up meant so much.

As we were able to momentarily experience, the reassuring, loving gift of touch!

5/4/22

Dig 4 Health

I had the chance to have a day each week in the prison garden. A day to treasure and look after my mental health with Eddie and the Dig 4 Health team. Today was my last visit so I wrote a poem for them.

A Dig 4 Health Pioneer- Yep, that was me! I'm so glad I joined Dig 4 Health.

Over eight months it improved my mental health and wealth.

Each week guaranteed me a day outside, a chance to learn and develop my patch with pride! Offered ears to listen and lots of support, a sanctuary, where it's ok to open up and talk.

A day away from the noise and commotion of the Wing, experiencing calm and quiet, with the joy that brings.

Sadly, soon it's my time to leave, Thanks to Dig 4 Health I'm proud of what I've been able to achieve!

I'll miss the garden and the 'boys' I leave behind.

Thanks to all those involved, I have a positive, calm state of mind.

So, I finish this poem with a thank you cheer, proud forever that I was a Dig 4 Health Pioneer!

6/4/22

A Note And Poem To Say "Thank You!"

Today marks the last day I will work in the library and see all four librarians. The last seven months have been a blast - a time when I have found the real me! This entry is a thank you note to all involved followed by a poem.

Well, I couldn't say Goodbye without a poem, but I want to leave you with one of my quotes. So, this is for the four of you, inspired by my time with you....

"The greatest wealth you can ever have, is to find peace with your own mental health."

Thank You

Thank you seems, such a small gesture,
When you four have helped me so much.

But, thank you said with emotion from
the heart within,

Carries more weight than I could ever
physically bring.

Thank you is more than anything what I
want to say,

For your kindness, support and guidance
every day.

Being the Library Orderly was the perfect
job for me,

My past is dealt with, I am at peace, I
have become free!

So, I finish this as it started, by saying,
For all you have done for me, it is a
forever Thank You!

7/4/22

Friday Feelings

Later today, I will find out if my
provisional HDC (tag) has been approved
and finalised for my release next Monday
11th April 2022.

As I wait, I feel

.Excited

.Anxious

.Nervous

.Happy

.Worried

.Relieved

.Apprehensive

and

.Ready!

But, if the news today doesn't go my way,
I will have a moments rest, dust myself off
and say to myself, "That's ok!"

Why?

Because, eventually my release will come
my way,

And when it does I will give thanks for the
arrival of that day!

8/4/22

Tag-Tastic!

Yesterday afternoon, (08/04/22) I received the following message...

Mr Loxton,

You are being released on HDC Mon 11/04/2022

Thanks, OMU (HDC)

I was blown away!!!!!

And, yesterday, I struggled to find the words to put it into context, the enormity of my feelings and the relief my time in Oakwood was nearly at an end!

Twenty-four hours on it is Saturday 9th April 2022 and although it won't feel completely real until I am in my brother's car on the other side of the gates, I do now believe that I only have two sleeps and one full day left!

On release day, you head towards admissions between 0745 and 0800. I have been told, the earlier you get there the better, as it depends how many are being released on that day as to how quickly I will be through the gates and free. For me, that's Monday 11th April 2022, a date etched into my soul!

So, how do I feel?

More than anything, I feel pride, relief and excitement.

Pride- in meeting and completing the challenges of prison.

Relief- I will have a Tag and can leave prison at the earliest opportunity.

Excitement- To see my family and friends!

Till tomorrow- it's time to sleep!

Final Full Day!

I woke early, to see a beautiful sunrise and morning frost. I still feel it hard to believe that I am actually going home tomorrow, but I'm allowing the lovely warm feelings to sink in!

I will endeavour to stay chilled and relaxed as much as possible to try to help keep the inevitable nerves and anxiety at bay.

This morning, I took my forty-five minutes exercise with Uncle. He was on the Wing when I arrived and from our initial chat we got on really well. He is one of the guys I hope to stay in touch with once I'm back outside. We have developed a strong friendship and I hope it will continue. I had an edible lunch, phoned my parents and then gifted Daz (a mate on the Wing) all the stuff I decided not to take home. It's the done thing in prison and it feels good to help a mate out!

This afternoon I've had my social time and then asked to 'bang up' so I could gather my thoughts. I will pack later this evening- it won't take long! I also have a final purple visit with my friend Michelle (half hour video call) It will be a perfect way to draw to a close my final day in prison. Her call is from 5 to 5.30 pm, which means by the time I get back to the Wing the other guys will all be 'banged up'. I would much rather have it that way, I don't seek or want fuss. I have said goodbye to those I need and want to.

The purple visit was fab! It was great to share my excitement of going home with my best friend! I've packed it didn't take long!

I enjoyed some chicken and salad from a mate in Kitchens and as my phone was still on, I've spoken to my brother - can't wait to see him in the morning!

It's now coming up to 10.30pm, just over an hour and a half and it will be my release day! I'm going to try and get some sleep if I can. When I wake it will be day three hundred and fifty-four of my prison sentence, but, more importantly, the day I get to leave Oakwood, ready to embrace the next chapter of my life, proud of what I have achieved during my time here!

10/4/22

From Oakwood To Home!

Well, it's 06.20am. I'm up, dressed, packed and ready to go!!!!!!

I managed a reasonable amount of sleep up until 04.20am, so I ended up watching a film on Greatest Movies called 'Precious Things'. Not great, but it passed the time!

As I write this I have Tipping Point on in the background. I look around my cell - my home for just short of forty weeks! It's the place I have spent nearly all of my ten months at Oakwood, the first four weeks being on the Beech Induction wing.

From a challenging start in this place, I have worked incredibly hard to rebuild myself. I will leave this cell with pride and a smile - grateful that I have found my way through it!

It has been an experience I never thought I'd have, or wanted to have, but for all its challenges, it has made me re-think, re-define and realise I have so much to look forward to. For that, I will be thankful of my time here.

You really do learn about yourself in the most unexpected of circumstances if you embrace it!

11/4/22

PART SEVEN

*Poems I've Written As I've
Adjusted To Being Home*

The Smile

Wherever you go, whatever you do, Carry a smile that's kind and true.

Share your smile as you travel life's way, as your smile WILL brighten a strangers day.

And as you give your smile out, leave yourself in no doubt, that by being smiley, happy and kind, you changed the mood of a strangers mind.

Because, as you smiled at the stranger who passed by,

His mood brightened and I know why....Because the stranger who received that smile was I.

The Weeping Willow

A poem I wrote for a tree, so beautiful and
inspiring to me.

The weeping willow taught me to cry,
Under the leaves I shed tears privately.

The weeping willow sweeps me in, as the
leaves rustle I hear the whisper 'you are
forgiven'.

The weeping willow standing proud and
tall, spreading love and hope to one and
all.

The weeping willow that stands in my
park, has been there for me when the
mood has been dark.

Today the weeping willow cast light all
around, as it whispered to me, "the path is

long with many twists. Dark times and bright times you'll see with me. Keep walking, exploring and sharing your thoughts, as I guide you to places where magic can be found".

The weeping willow my beloved, inspiring tree, guiding, listening and showing the light, that helps me feel free.

As The Night Falls..

As night falls, and your bed calls, However you felt your day went, it's time to put it in the box marked spent.

Because today is nearly done, and whatever it threw at you has been overcome.

So as you lay down to rest, be proud because you gave your best.

Close your eyes and let dreams drift in,
the day is done and that's a win.

And that is what really matters, as until
you wake, who knows what tomorrow will
bring.

Anxiety Called

I stood rooted to the spot, breathing
increasing, heart beat racing.

The physical sickness was palpable, as
sweat poured down my brow.

So hot and shaky I did feel, but inside I
felt cold, so cold.

Inside my mind all I felt was panic, I
turned and left when I was able.

As I sit and write this at home, Although
I'm a bit down on me.

I tried, I'll try again and why?

Because I'm learning how to be,
Accepting anxiety is part of me.

There will be challenges along the way,
But that's the beauty of living each day.

Sleepless Nights

One of the hardest things I find, is
switching off an active mind.

All I want to do is sleep, but thoughts at
night hit hard and deep.

Worries and doubts circle around, as I
look for any peace to be found.

Questions and fears invade my brain,

Rattling through like the night freight
train.

Thought voices get louder and louder,
Which leads to a real mood downer.

Tonight it is a struggle to sleep, so tired
are my eyes they start to weep.

Fingers crossed it won't be long, until I'm
dreaming a sleepy song.

War In My Head

Suddenly I'm hit,

Mind pain drives me to the ground,

My thoughts bleeding out.

Bangs echo so loud,

Like grenades within my head,

Exploding my brain.

Carefully I crawl,

Searching for peace from the din,

Of war all around.

I raise a white flag,

In the hope of a ceasefire,

To silence my mind.

This war is cruel,

The war I fight no one sees.

Hidden from your view.

But fight it I will,

As I am worth fighting for,

To find peace for me.

You And I

I am me,

You are you,

That's the way it's always been.

We might look different,

We might speak differently, but we both
have a heart no one can see.

I don't know your pain,

You don't know mine,

But should I judge you or just be kind?

It's kindness for me every time,

As the words we speak,

And the actions we take,

Change lives, so let's change them for the
better by being kind.

Feeling Blue

Sometimes when you feel blue,

Your mind torments and screams 'I hate
you'.

You question why you feel this way,

When yesterday was a decent day.

That's one of the anomalies of mental
health,

It can deliver a blow as if by stealth.

There's no easy explanation for why this
happens,

Mental illness is invisible, no signs, no
patterns.

On difficult days I wonder how my mind
is wired,

As even thinking leaves me incredibly
tired.

But now when I feel this way,

I say 'these feeling are, survivable and
okay'.

Accept these feelings, Accept these thoughts,

Then smile and say 'well done me for getting through'.

Be proud you did and tomorrow start the day by being kind to YOU.

Words On Friends

Some friends come, some friends go, But every friend you've met in life,

Will have helped you navigate hope and strife.

Some friends are forever, some are special for the time had together, but whether they are friends now or yesterday, those friends helped you find your way.

Some friends you won't yet know, You'll meet them when they can help you to grow.

So for friends no more, friends forever and friends not yet met,

Be grateful for them all as we owe them a thank you debt.

A debt of thanks for helping us through, as when we needed them most....

Friends have, and always will be there for me and you.

The Cruel Mind (My Mind On The Worst Of Days)

Fearful, scared, out of my mind, wishing my mind would find a way to be kind.

I decided for everyone I held dear, there lives would be better if I wasn't here.

I felt I had nothing left to give, but if I took my life would they find a way to forgive?

In the dead of night I'd sneak downstairs and weep, tormented by thoughts that wouldn't let me sleep.

Tortured by the voices deep inside my head, silently screaming I'd be better off dead.

As my thoughts got ever more cruel, it was like fighting myself in a deadly duel.

In my head the way to win, was to stop breathing, to finally give in.

I wasn't thinking about anyone else, I needed to end the pain for myself.

At my worst that was my cruel mind.

Today I'm learning to be 'mind kind',
And I'm grateful I didn't go through with
my suicide.

PART EIGHT

Three Months on!

Today, Monday 11th July 2022, marks three months since my prison release.

Until now, I hadn't planned to add anymore to my little book, but today I have been reminded that in one day you can experience both happiness and sadness as you travel on the journey of life. This has presented me with the opportunity to offer up a few final points. Some may help, some may not, but it feels the right time to share them, to mark three months on.

I wish you well on your journey. Stay strong, as I know you all are, and remember - in living, you can surprise yourself. I did and each and every day I am grateful to be alive.

Go well, stay strong and stay safe.

11/7/2

PART NINE

*In Conclusion- My Five
Points for Living*

1.   You can only control certain things, for example; the time you get up, what you might eat, which friend you may call that day. You can't control the changes to your plans, whether your friend answers your call, world events, or, in my case, believing that if I was kind to others, put myself last and always offered support to others that my football team would win! So today, and everyday only try and control what you can actually control.

2.   If a friendship fails, a marriage breaks down or a trust is broken it is NEVER just your fault.

3.   Don't catastrophize! I have and I still can be quite guilty of this. If I don't hear from someone after contacting them I can think I have said something to upset them and the friendship maybe lost

forever. People have busy lives, trust that they are there for you, and show patience, you have no reason to doubt the loss of the friendship, other than the worry of your own mind. Be patient, wait for the facts. When I wait I often find my worrying is misplaced.

4.	Find activities and distractions to ground you. Have a Mental Toolkit for those challenging moments. Some of my favourites include...

•	Walking- I try to manage 3 miles a day, but do whatever you can, the power of nature and fresh air can change the day and lift your mood.

•	Reading - books can be a great distraction. For me it is non-fiction books, especially those about personal well-being. They can make you realise you are not alone. That was certainly the case for me during my time in prison.

- Writing - no rules or method. I write what I want when I want. Sometimes I share, sometimes I don't. Getting thoughts down on paper really helps me and sometimes writing can be better than talking. I for one find writing cathartic and an easier way to process my anxious thoughts. Often once on paper, I read my thoughts back and realise those thoughts were not as bad as first thought or feared.

- Music, create playlists for your moods. It is the words of every song I select that does it for me. The power is in the words, whatever the mood might be.

- Try to avoid, or limit things that make you feel ungrounded. For me, it is news intake and social media. I try to limit my news access to one broadcast a day. When I do I am definitely less anxious for it, news by its nature is stressful!!! Why would you keep going back to what is causing you anxiety and stress?

5.   Reach out, talk, send a text, letter, or pick up the phone but find a way to ask for help. You deserve that help, whatever your mind might say. After all in making that plea, you are starting to allow yourself to be you, and with that you can find acceptance, contentment and happiness. Something each and everyone of us is worthy of, even on difficult days.

And finally try to remember this....

"You will have offered more to others than you will ever know just by being kind to yourself and by being YOU!"

11/7/22

Credits